A CAT'S
LITTLE INSTRUCTION
BOOK

Also available from Thorsons

LIFE'S LITTLE INSTRUCTION BOOK
LIFE'S LITTLE INSTRUCTION BOOK, VOLUME II
by
H. Jackson Brown Jr

A CAT'S LITTLE INSTRUCTION BOOK

Leigh W. Rutledge

Pandora

An Imprint of HarperCollins*Publishers*

Thorsons
An Imprint of HarperCollins*Publishers*
77-85 Fulham Palace Road,
Hammersmith, London, W6 8JB

First published by Dutton, NAL, Penguin Books USA,
375 Hudson Street, New York, NY 10014, 1993
Published by Thorsons 1993
1 3 5 7 9 10 8 6 4 2

A catalogue record for this book
is available from the British Library

ISBN 0 7225 2921 X

Printed in Great Britain by
HarperCollinsManufacturing Glasgow

To Beardsley, Spitfire and Dr Tom Bird

🐾 Always lick after meals

🐾 When in doubt, chase something

🐾 Keep your tail away from stoves, candles,
lit cigarettes, automatic dishwasher doors,
children, rocking-chairs and dogs. God only
gave you one tail – take good care of it

🐾 Worry about courage, cleanliness and furballs

🐾 *Don't* worry about what other cats think of you. Remember, the cats who often do the most with their lives are the ones who were laughed at, ridiculed or made fun of as kittens

❖ Be adorable

❖ Stay out of car engines

❖ Stay out of open windows during
thunderstorms

❖ Stay indoors on Bonfire Night

🐾   Surprise someone by hiding
in the laundry basket

- Avoid the temptation to spend all day waiting expectantly by the birdbath

- Christmas trees are meant to be climbed

- Long naps never go out of fashion

- Just say no to catnip

🐾 The three Great Lies of Life are:

1 The cheque is in the post
2 All I want is one kiss
3 It'll be all right, just get in the
   travelling basket

🐾 Avoid cleaning your private parts in public places

🐾 Forgive your enemies – but hit them a couple of times first

🐾 Never go to a vet who doesn't have
cats himself

🐾 Never go back to a vet who discusses his
or her stock portfolio while taking your
temperature

❖ Always make sure the lid is down
on the toilet before jumping on it

🐾 Don't run to the vet's for every little ache and pain. Ninety percent of your medical problems will get better on their own, regardless of what you take or do for them

🐾 Remember, no matter how much they love you, all human beings are biased towards their own species

🐾 Never go to bed with a resentful heart or a dirty face

🐾 Learn to recognise the sound of a bowl being filled with cereal; milk usually follows

🐾   Be astonishingly mysterious

❖ Look *in* to people as well as *at* them

❖ When depressed or confused, try lying on your back with your legs in the air; sometimes the world just looks better upside-down

🐾 Never be afraid to seek centre stage

🐾 No matter what you've done wrong, always try to make it look like the dog did it

🐾 Sniff every stranger

🐾 Never take a nap in a parked car – you may wake up and find yourself being carried off to a faraway place

🐾 Don't eat anti-freeze, tinsel, broken Christmas-tree ornaments, straight pins, paper clips, strange pills lying on the bathroom floor, polystyrene or mice you suspect have just eaten rat poison

❖ Cuddle someone you love on snowy afternoons

❖ Sleep in a flowerbed to stay cool on hot summer days

🐾 Help with jigsaw puzzles

🐾 Avoid like the plague any person who has, within the last 12 months, picked you up and shaken you adoringly

🐾 When a friend wants to lick you, let them

🐾 Never brood about the past. If you're ever tempted to, take a good hard look at the humans around you. They do it all the time – are *they* happy?

❖ Forgive people who babble baby-talk in your face. They're only repeating what someone else taught them

❖ Learn the difference between idleness and repose – one wastes time, the other luxuriates in it

🐾 When playing games with your own kittens, let them get the better of you

🐾 When playing games with someone else's kittens, beat them up

❖ Be a friend to people who have suffered grief, rejection, abuse, financial loss or recent illness. In moments of personal tragedy, human beings tend to run away from one another – learn from their bad example

❦ Never ever let anyone floss your teeth unless you're unconscious or dead

❦ Let sleeping dogs lie – literally

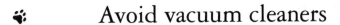 Avoid vacuum cleaners

❖ Stay off diving boards

❖ Get your booster shots every year

❖ Take time to savour the view from every window in your house

❖ Never chew on electrical cords or wires

🐾 Begin each day with a long hard stretch

🐾 Never sleep too close to a fireplace that has a fire going in it

🐾 Remember that foxes, skunks and owls usually have the last word in any confrontation

🐾 Leave every dog with the impression that you are a lion cub who will be back to get even when you grow up

❧ Never eat raw meat or stale leftovers. Always ask yourself: if it isn't something humans would feed their kids, why are they feeding it to *you*?

🐾   It's only an old wives' tale that a little
litter tossed out of the cat box wards off
the Devil. Make an effort to keep the area
around your cat box clean

🐾 Don't sit or sleep on the microwave when it's in operation. You don't know *what* it might be doing to you

🐾 Watch out for human feet. (They won't watch out for you)

❖ Don't bite your nails

❖ Choose your loyalties carefully, but once you've chosen them put your heart and soul into them

❖   Always clean between your toes

❖ Ignore any and all silly propaganda about cats being aloof, amoral, sinister, stupid and false-hearted. The people who believe such things are themselves more often than not aloof, amoral, sinister, stupid and false-hearted

🐾 Run away and hide the moment you hear any group of human beings speculating about whether cats always land on their feet

🐾 Become a force to be reckoned with – but don't run it into the ground

🐾   Stay out of the rain

🐾   Stay out of the snow

🐾   Stay out of the tumble dryer

🐾 Seek out good hiding places

🐾 Look both ways before crossing the street. Never *dart*. Better yet, don't cross streets

❖ Treat yourself to a nap in the sock drawer once in a while

❖ When climbing trees, never be satisfied with the lowest limb. However, bear in mind that most firemen have better things to do than get cats out of trees. If you get stuck, you're pretty much on your own

🐾 Avoid packs of roving children. A child alone can sometimes be dealt with, but once in a herd they often turn into berserk little creatures trying to impress one another

❖ Explore your territory, but don't become a fanatic about marking it

❖ Roll in the dirt at least once a week to maintain a healthy and beautiful coat

🐾 After the age of ten, have your teeth checked regularly

🐾 Learn the difference between a pair of shoes and a litter box

🐾 Never worry about vet's or cat food bills. Someone else will pay them

🐾 Don't be fooled by cat furniture – tiny beds, cramped baskets, etc. – sold in pet shops. Human furniture is always more plush and comfortable

❖ Let your emotions get the best of you sometimes

❖ Cultivate bedroom eyes when asking for things. If you're ignored, don't be afraid to put a little bit of claw into your request

🐾 Climb the living room curtains to develop upper-body strength

🐾 Resist an urge to leap onto the ceiling fan, especially when it's in motion

- Own nothing, and be owned by no one

- Chase and bite human toes through the bedcovers

❖ Remember that every baby bird you encounter has a mother who would be heartbroken if you ate it

❖ Never be discouraged by the words No,
Stop that, or Bad Cat

❖ Never be overly concerned when someone
screams, If you ever do that again, I'm
going to make you live outside! It's almost
always an idle threat

❖   To make a lasting impression at parties, sit in the onion dip or stick your head in the punchbowl and start slurping loudly. If all else fails, perch yourself like a vulture on the arm of a sofa and leave all the guests with the impression that if they don't finish the hors d'oeuvres soon, *you* will

❧ Never try to stick your head through
any opening that your whiskers won't
clear easily

❧ Ignore any endeavour whose primary goal
is self-improvement

🐾 Don't worry about little things

🐾 Don't worry about big things

🐾 Surprise the entire household by unrolling all the toilet paper at night

🐾 Never purr half-heartedly

🐾 Never yawn half-heartedly

🐾 Never eat more than your own weight
in table scraps

🐾 Spurn kitty clothes

🐾 Never let anyone dye your hair a funny colour or give you a trendy haircut

🐾 Eschew coloured bows or plastic barettes

- Ignore all fitness fads

- Say Yes! to armchairs, cut flowers, stomach tickling and tuna fish

🐾 Inspire whimsy in everyone
you meet

🐾 Remember – meow and the world meows with you; hiss and you hiss alone

🐾 Force people to throw you off their laps at least three times before conceding that they actually mean it

- Take time to sit in the grass and watch the clouds roll by

- Chase butterflies

- No matter how old you are, never be afraid to express the kitten within

Don't play in plastic bags

❧ Keep in mind that just because a man or woman is poor or even homeless it doesn't mean they can't be a loving and devoted companion. There is absolutely *no* correlation between money and a good heart

🐾 Refuse to retrieve things

🐾 Protest loudly if anyone ever suggests getting a new puppy

Keep everybody's secrets

🐾 Ignore your mistakes

🐾 Scratch your ears regularly

🐾 Pose for photos

❦ Bath with a friend

❦ Learn to watch everything, even with
   your eyes closed

🐾 Never join anything

🐾 Persuade people to devote their free
time to petting you

❧ Steer clear of wasps, bees, ants and spiders. At best, they make iffy playmates; at worst, they're hazardous between-meal snacks

🐾 The three best rainy day activities are:

1 Sleeping

2 Napping

3 Taking it easy

🐾 The three best late night activities are:

1 Chasing a ping-pong ball around the bathtub
2 Dragging underwear, tights and socks from room to room
3 Climbing and hanging from the blinds while wailing loudly

Be suspicious of anyone whose clothes
are immaculate and completely free of cat
hairs. It means they either don't like cats
or don't hug the ones they have

🐾 Be inscrutable

🐾 Be regal

🐾 Be nobody's fool

🐾 Don't waste time watching television

🐾 Don't waste time staring in mirrors

🐾 Don't waste time trying to figure out the meaning of life

❧ Don't introduce yourself to new neighbours
by sharpening your claws on their patio
furniture or playing in their flowerbeds.
First impressions can rarely be undone

🐾 When in doubt, let your tail do the talking

🐾 Drink lots of water

🐾 Play and sleep in cardboard boxes

🐾 Resist any impulse to fall asleep in
your food dish

🐾 For mild stomach upsets, eat plenty of grass. If that fails, try a little yoghurt

🐾 Make friends with the milkman

🐾 Help with making the bed

🐾 Help with re-decorating, even if no
one asks you

🐾 Help with making dinner

❖ To stay warm on cold winter days, sleep on the sill of an east window in the morning and a west window in the afternoon. That way, you'll always catch the sunshine

🐾 Refuse to tolerate being locked out of
the bedroom for any reason whatsoever

🐾 Moult a lot

❖ Control your temper

❖ Avoid acting on jealous impulses, no matter how justified they seem at the time

🐾 Try not to sit around with your tongue sticking half out of your mouth; it looks ridiculous

🐾 Beware of guns

🐾 Avoid second-hand cigarette smoke

🐾 When kneading someone's stomach, stop just short of drawing blood

 Push your luck

🐾 Don't wait until Christmas Day to open the presents

🐾 Don't whine when your toys disappear under the refrigerator or down the heating ducts. Accept the fact that life can be brutally unfair at times

🐾 Never make abrupt moves. Always *insinuate* yourself into any situation, including a warm lap

🐾 Regard all neatly stacked piles of paper as provocation

- Don't just inhabit a house; become its *soul*

- Learn to develop a memorable meow

- Find any excuse to run up and down the stairs dementedly

🐾 Retain your sense of wonder about all things

🐾 Retain your curiosity

🐾 Refrain from giving anyone a dead mouse or
bird as a present; your idea of the perfect gift
may not be somebody else's

🐾 Don't throw yourself at house guests, no matter how receptive they seem; it compromises your dignity

🐾 Steer clear of cacti

🐾 Never eat pork

🐾 Never run across a recently mopped floor; you could slip and hurt yourself

🐾 Don't cry over spilt milk – lap it up instead

🐾 Bestow love bites sparingly and only to those who will understand the spirit in which they were meant

🐾 Always look astonished when you break something, even if you meant to do it

🐾 Always sleep under the covers. Humans will never throw you out if you snuggle under the covers with them

🐾 Stay out of rubbish bins and skips unless you or someone you love is starving

🐾 Avoid chewing on pens or pencils; the ink and lead could poison you

🐾 Resist the temptation to claw strangers who make dense remarks like 'Isn't it amazing? Every cat almost has its own personality'

- If you ever find yourself homeless, remember: look pathetic, not sickly. You want to inspire sympathy, not visions of vet's bills. And don't forget to purr disarmingly

- Lay claim to every jacket, sweater and shirt as soon as it lands on a chair

🐾 Don't waste time learning to do things that others will do for you

🐾 When a child starts screaming or crying loudly, resist the temptation to sit on its face

🐾 Become a paragon of sanity, sensuality and contentment

- Never take food right out of someone else's mouth – unless you're absolutely convinced they won't retaliate

- Never retract your claws completely, except with your very best friends

- Never bite the hand that feeds you – except as a last resort

- Never try to be something you're not

- Never give in to vulgarity

- Never be too smart for your own good

🐾 Trust your intuition

🐾 Tread silently

🐾 Knock small things off counters

❖ Avoid shoving your private parts in people's faces, no matter how well you think you know them

🐾 Always enter a room with poise and confidence. If you accidentally slip or stumble, stop immediately. Start licking yourself rigorously – it distracts would-be hecklers

🐾 Learn to recognize the difference between ordinary cans being opened and cat food cans being opened

🐾 Chase all shoelaces

🐾 If someone breaks into the house when
no one else is there, hide. Leave the heroics
to dogs

🐾 Remember: everyone likes to wake up
to a kiss

🐾 Sleep under table lamps

🐾 Sleep on the answering machine

🐾 Sleep in the middle of the hall

❧ Be bold

❧ Be winsome

❧ Be wildly tender

❧ Autumn leaves and newspapers were made to be played in

❧ Sleeping in the sunlight is often the best medicine for whatever ails you

❧ Make the world your scratching post

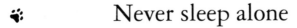 Never sleep alone

🐾   Become someone's friend for life